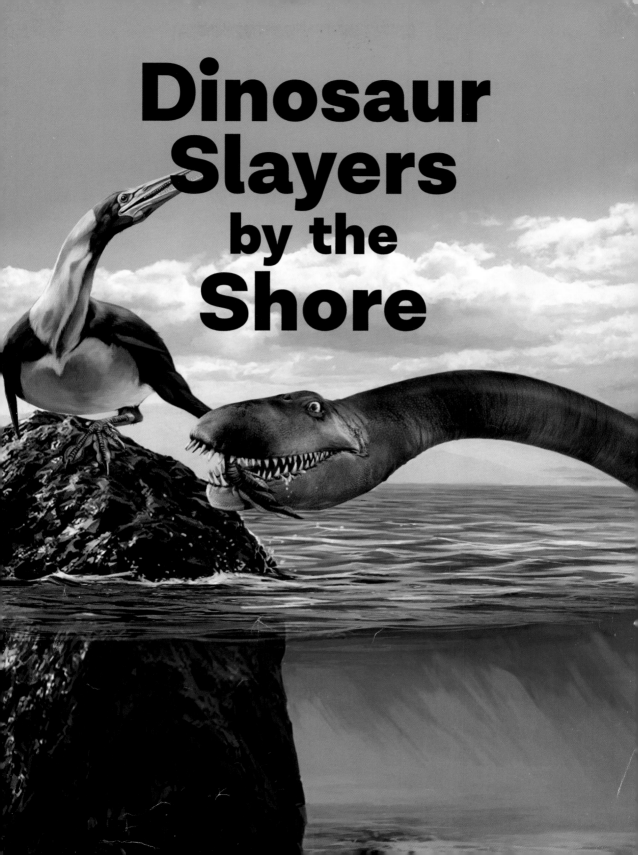

Dinosaur Slayers
by the
Shore

Thanks to the creative team:
Senior Editor: Alice Peebles
Consultant: Neil Clark
Design: Perfect Bound Ltd

Hungry Tomato®
A division of Lerner Publishing Group, Inc.
241 First Avenue North
Minneapolis, MN 55401 USA

For reading levels and more information, look up
this title at www.lernerbooks.com.

Main body text set in Graviola Soft 12/14.

Library of Congress Cataloging-in-Publication Data

Names: Mason, Paul, 1967– author. | Leonard, Andre, 1954– illustrator.
Title: Dinosaur slayers by the shore / Paul Mason ; Andre Leonard, [illustrator].
Description: Minneapolis : Hungry Tomato, [2018] | Series: Dinosaurs rule | Audience: Ages 8–12. | Audience: Grades 4 to 6.
Identifiers: LCCN 2018006925 (print) | LCCN 2018010805 (ebook) | ISBN 9781541523999 (eb pdf) | ISBN 9781541501034 (lb : alk. paper)
Subjects: LCSH: Dinosaurs—Juvenile literature. | Dinosaurs—Behavior—Juvenile literature.
Classification: LCC QE861.5 (ebook) | LCC QE861.5 M342978 2018 (print) | DDC 567.9—dc23

LC record available at https://lccn.loc.gov/2018006925

Manufactured in the United States of America
1-43774-33632-4/19/2018

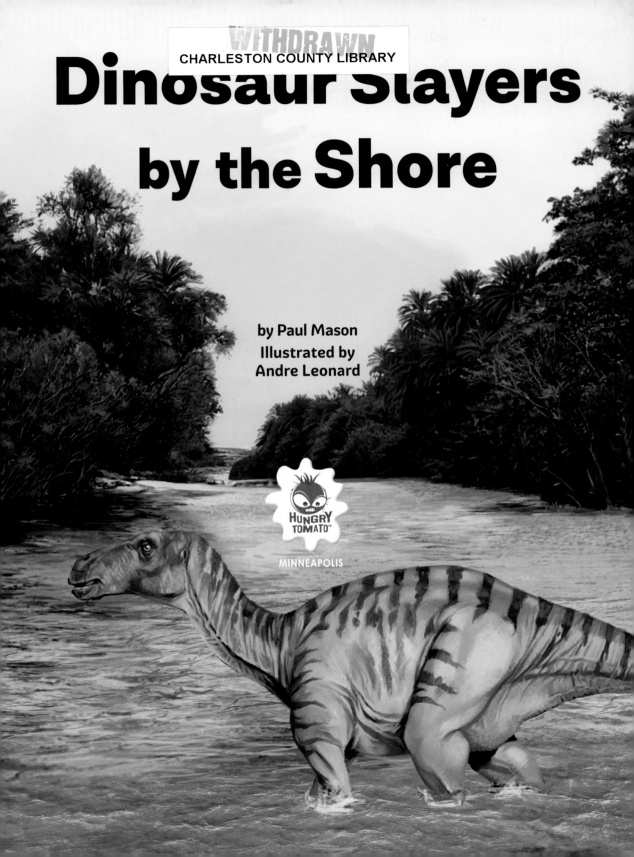

Dinosaur Slayers by the Shore

by Paul Mason

Illustrated by
Andre Leonard

HUNGRY TOMATO™

MINNEAPOLIS

Contents

Reptile Rulers

Dinosaurs walked the earth for nearly 200 million years. For their last 79 million years (the Cretaceous Period), dinosaurs were dominant. They really did rule the earth.

Practically wherever there was land, there were dinosaurs. Many of them lived on the shores of the sea or around river estuaries, where they could find plenty to eat.

Triassic world

(250–201 million years ago)

A "supercontinent" called Pangaea was the main land during the Triassic Period. With only one giant landmass, there were fewer coastlines than later.

Jurassic world

(201–145 million years ago)

At this time Pangaea began to break up and form new lands. The amount of coastline increased. New rivers flowed into the seas, forming estuaries and floodplains.

Cretaceous world

(145–66 million years ago)

During the Cretaceous Period, the continents we know today began to form. There were more coastlines and rivers than ever before.

A Two-Course Lunch
Baryonyx vs. *Iguanodon*

Baryonyx thought it had already caught its lunch—some tasty sturgeon. Now, though, a family of *Iguanodon* has started to cross the river. The young one especially would make an excellent meal.

The plant eaters turn back—but *Baryonyx* has seen them. It may already be too late to escape!

Baryonyx

Baryonyx hunted mainly in river deltas, the wide places where rivers flow into the sea. It had a long, shallow head, a stretched-out snout, and long, cone-like teeth. Once a fish got caught on these, it could not wriggle free.

At over 2 .2 tons (2 t), *Baryonyx* was a large dinosaur. As well as fish, it sometimes hunted bigger prey.

KILLER FACT

Baryonyx means "heavy claw" in Latin. Its name comes from the large claw on the dinosaur's first finger.

Spinosaur
Baryonyx was from a family of predators called spinosaurs, which all had a raised ridge along their back.

Grippers
Hooked claws helped it grip wriggly fish.

FACT FILE

Alive: 129–125 million years ago
Order and Family: Saurischia/ Spinosauridae
Length: 24 ft. (7.5 m)
Height: 8 ft. 6 in. (2.6 m)
Weight: 1.3 tons (1.2 t)
Diet: carnivorous
Fossils found: parts of a skull and skeleton
Location: southeast England

Iguanodon

A large *Iguanodon* weighed more than 3.3 tons (3 t), so it was a big dinosaur—but not particularly well armed. Its hands were equipped with a large thumb spike, but it isn't clear whether *Iguanodon* used this as a weapon.

For protection, *Iguanodon* probably traveled in herds. When these dinosaurs moved in search of food, their herds may have numbered thousands of animals.

KILLER FACT

Iguanodon often walked on four legs, but to escape a predator it probably ran on its more powerful back legs.

FACT FILE

Alive: 155–126 million years ago
Order: Ornithischia
Length: 33 ft. (10 m), maybe longer
Height: 11 ft. (3.5 m)
Weight: 3. 5 tons (3.2 t)
Diet: herbivorous
Fossils found: many complete skulls and skeletons
Location: southeast England; Belgium

Low speed
Iguanodon was a heavy dinosaur, and not particularly fast moving—especially when accompanied by young.

Battle on the Bank
Spinosaurus vs. *Carcharodontosaurus*

Carcharodontosaurus has had a very nasty surprise. It came to the water's edge for a drink and accidentally strayed into the territory of a giant predator—*Spinosaurus*.

Spinosaurus is bigger than *Carcharodontosaurus* but not as powerful. This sudden fight might just end in a draw!

Spinosaurus

Spinosaurus often hunted in coastal mangrove forests. The most noticeable thing about it is the huge, sail-like fin sticking up from its spine.

No one is sure what the sail was for. It may have been for attracting a mate, regulating temperature, storing fat (like a camel's hump), or swimming (like a shark's fin).

Biggest predator?
Experts think *Spinosaurus* was one of the biggest predatory dinosaurs ever.

SCALE

Hungry hunter
Spinosaurus mostly ate small dinosaurs and fish but could take on bigger prey.

KILLER FACT
Spinosaurus may have had pressure receptors inside its snout so it could sense prey without seeing it—for example, with its face underwater.

Carcharodontosaurus

Carcharodontosaurus was a big predator, used to taking on enormous dinosaurs. Its prey included the giant titanosaur *Paralititan*, which could weigh 22 tons (20 t).

Even among the tiny-brained dinosaurs, though, *Carcharodontosaurus* may not have been the smartest. Despite being bigger than *Tyrannosaurus*, *Carcharodontosaurus* probably had an even smaller brain.

SCALE

Mighty ancestor
Experts think *Carcharodontosaurus* was descended from *Allosaurus*, an apex predator of the late Jurassic Period.

FACT FILE

Alive: 112–93 million years ago
Order and Family: Saurischia/ Carcharodontosauridae
Length: 39 ft. (12 m)
Height: 11 ft. (3.5 m)
Weight: 5.5 tons (5 t)
Diet: carnivorous
Fossils found: a partial skull and parts of a skeleton
Location: Egypt

Bombed to bits
The first specimen ever found was stored in a German museum—but it was destroyed in an Allied bombing raid in World War II.

KILLER FACT
Sometimes called the "shark-toothed dinosaur," *Carcharodontosaurus* had long, sharp teeth with serrated edges like a bread knife for slicing into flesh.

Run For It!
Majungasaurus vs. *Masiakasaurus*

Masiakasaurus had better not finish this meal—it needs to get moving! If *Majungasaurus* gets a grip on a victim, it rarely lets go.

Zig-zagging as it runs away might help *Masiakasaurus* escape: *Majungasaurus* is not very good at making side-to-side movements.

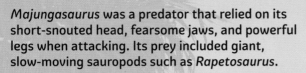

Majungasaurus

Majungasaurus was a predator that relied on its short-snouted head, fearsome jaws, and powerful legs when attacking. Its prey included giant, slow-moving sauropods such as *Rapetosaurus*.

Majungasaurus had surprisingly small, weak arms, even compared to other weedy-armed predators in the dinosaur world. Its fingers were fused together, with claws sticking out at the end.

KILLER FACT

Some experts think *Majungasaurus* may have bitten its prey, then held on like a bulldog, waiting for its victim to weaken.

FACT FILE

Alive: 70–66 million years ago
Order and Family: Saurischia/ Abelisauridae
Length: 20 ft. (6 m)
Height: 7 ft. 2 in. (2.2 m)
Weight: 1,650 lb. (750 kg)
Diet: carnivorous
Fossils found: a skull and most parts of skeleton, so almost every part of this dinosaur is known
Location: Madagascar

Show-off
The spike on its head was made of lightweight material, so experts think *Majungasaurus* probably used it for show.

Toppling over
Fossils suggest this dinosaur did not have good balance. Sudden sideways movements while running might even have toppled it over.

SCALE

Masiakasaurus

KILLER FACT

Because *Masiakasaurus*'s front teeth stuck out so much, prey that thought it had escaped was sometimes caught.

Masiakasaurus was a small predatory dinosaur about the size of a big dog. Its most noticeable feature was its teeth. They poked out crazily in front of the dinosaur's mouth from both its upper and lower jaws.

The teeth were long and slightly spoon-shaped and probably helped *Masiakasaurus* grip small prey—but they would have been little use against a predator like *Majungasaurus*.

FACT FILE

Alive: 70–66 million years ago
Order and Family: Saurischia/ Noasauridae
Length: 6 ft. 6 in. (2 m)
Height: 1 ft. 6 in. (0.5 m)
Weight: 44 lb. (20 kg)
Diet: carnivorous
Fossils found: parts of a skull and skeleton
Location: Madagascar

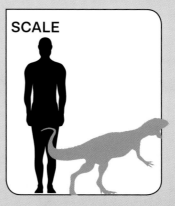

SCALE

Slicing flesh
The front teeth were for gripping, but the sharp back teeth were designed for slicing into flesh.

Ambush from the Water!

Sarcosuchus vs. *Nigersaurus*

What seemed like a peaceful place for a drink has turned out to be anything but!

Nigersaurus checked for land predators before coming down to the water's edge, but it couldn't check below the surface—and that's where the giant crocodile *Sarcosuchus* was lurking.

Sarcosuchus

A large *Sarcosuchus* probably ate just about anything that came close enough. In the water it may have hunted *Mawsonia*, a giant fish.

At the water's edge, *Sarcosuchus* probably leapt out at animals that had come to drink or attacked those trying to cross rivers and estuaries. Few if any dinosaurs could go near the water without fear of *Sarcosuchus*.

FACT FILE

Alive: 112 million years ago
Class and Family: Reptilia/ Pholidosauridae
Length: 39 ft. (12 m)
Height: 4 ft. (1.2 m)
Weight: 8.8 tons (8 t)
Diet: carnivorous
Fossils found: an almost-complete skull, most parts of skeleton
Location: Mali; Algeria; Niger; Brazil

SCALE

Nose knobble
The bulge on the nose is called a bulla. It may have been for smelling, making a noise, or some other use.

KILLER FACT

Sarcosuchus was twice the size of the largest, most dangerous crocodile of today, the saltwater crocodile.

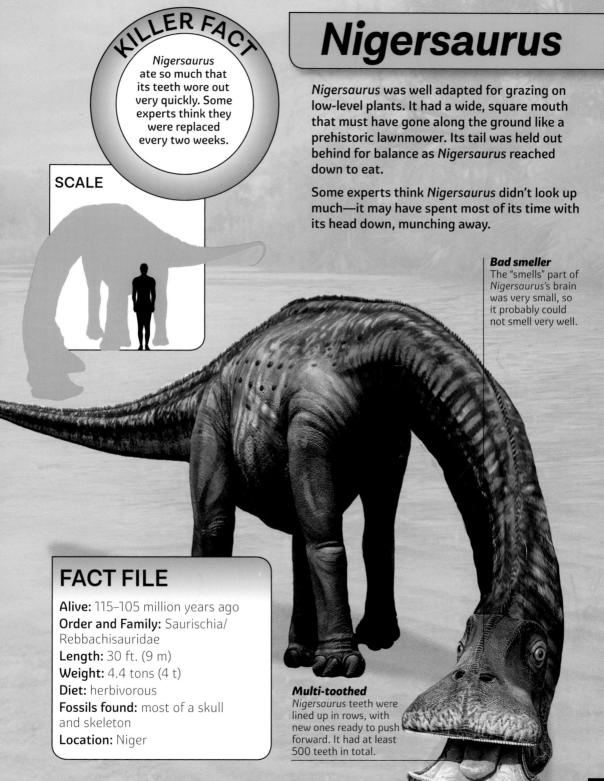

Nigersaurus

Nigersaurus was well adapted for grazing on low-level plants. It had a wide, square mouth that must have gone along the ground like a prehistoric lawnmower. Its tail was held out behind for balance as *Nigersaurus* reached down to eat.

Some experts think *Nigersaurus* didn't look up much—it may have spent most of its time with its head down, munching away.

SCALE

Bad smeller
The "smells" part of *Nigersaurus*'s brain was very small, so it probably could not smell very well.

FACT FILE

Alive: 115–105 million years ago
Order and Family: Saurischia/Rebbachisauridae
Length: 30 ft. (9 m)
Weight: 4.4 tons (4 t)
Diet: herbivorous
Fossils found: most of a skull and skeleton
Location: Niger

Multi-toothed
Nigersaurus teeth were lined up in rows, with new ones ready to push forward. It had at least 500 teeth in total.

Attack from Below!

Albertonectes vs. *Hesperornis*

Hesperornis was just about to dive after a fish when it felt a tug on its wing tip—and this tug could spell death. If *Albertonectes* gets a good grip with its sharp teeth, *Hesperornis* is unlikely to escape.

Albertonectes

Albertonectes was a marine reptile, not a dinosaur. It was a good swimmer and used all four of its paddles to "fly" through the water.

The most astounding feature of this dinosaur was its neck. Long-necked swimming reptiles such as *Albertonectes* are called elasmosaurs. Their long necks probably helped them to catch fish more easily. *Albertonectes*'s neck was the longest of all the elasmosaurs.

Bone numbers
With 76 neck vertebrae, *Albertonectes* had more neck bones than any other elasmosaur.

SCALE

FACT FILE

Alive: 74+ million years ago
Order and Family: Plesiosauria/ Elasmosauridae
Length: 37 ft. 8 in. (11.5 m)
Weight: 2.2+ tons (2+ t)
Diet: mainly fish
Fossils found: a spine and most of the rest of a skeleton
Location: Alberta, Canada

Hesperornis

Fishing bird
Its long neck helped *Hesperornis* catch fish, its main food.

Toothy beak
Like other early birds, *Hesperornis* had teeth inside its beak for holding on to wriggly fish.

Hesperornis could not fly, but it was a strong, graceful swimmer. It powered through the water using its strong legs and webbed feet. Its wings were small and streamlined and may have been used for steering.

The shallow, warm seas where this bird hunted were full of fish—and predators. Among the most fearsome were the mosasaurs: huge, toothed swimming reptiles that ate anything in their path.

KILLER FACT

On land *Hespornis* found moving about difficult. It moved in a wobbly shuffle at best and may even have had to push itself along on its belly.

SCALE

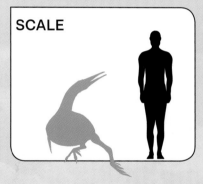

FACT FILE

Alive: 84–78 million years ago
Family: Hesperornithidae
Length: 6 ft. (1.8 m)
Height: 3 ft. 3 in. (1 m), standing
Weight: 18 lb. (8 kg)
Diet: carnivorous
Fossils found: skulls and skeletons, so almost everything about this bird is known
Location: central United States; central Canada

Believe It or Not!

Spinosaurus was the biggest predator

Tyrannosaurus might be more famous, *Allosaurus* might have been more vicious—but it was *Spinosaurus* that was the biggest predatory dinosaur.

Only a few remains have been found, though, and some experts think there might be an even bigger *Spinosaurus* out there, waiting to be discovered.

Rock band dinosaur

Masiakasaurus's full name is *Masiakasaurus knopfleri*. The people who discovered the dinosaur really liked the band Dire Straits—so they named it after the lead singer, Mark Knopfler.

Sound traveled farther in dinosaur oceans

Predators in the dinosaur-era seas would have been able to hear splashing noises from twice as far away as today's ocean predators.

This is because the seawater back then was more acidic, and sound travels farther in acidic water.

Sarcosuchus never grew up

The giant crocodile *Sarcosuchus* may never have stopped growing throughout its entire life. One fossil of a 40-year-old *Sarcosuchus* showed that it was *still* not fully grown!

Hesperornis must have had terrible breath

This early bird had small holes in the roof of its mouth. The long teeth in its lower jaw fitted inside these when its beak was closed.

With rotting bits of fish trapped in these holes, *Hesperornis's* breath must have been strong enough to knock you down!

What really killed the dinosaurs?

At the end of the Cretaceous Period, the dinosaurs were wiped out. Many people think an asteroid crash or super volcanic eruption caused a long winter the dinosaurs couldn't survive.

A few people, though, think changing sea levels might have been to blame.

As sea levels fell at the end of the Cretaceous, many shorelines—such as North America's inland sea—disappeared. The dinosaurs could not adapt to the changing world and died off.

What Were Dinosaurs Really Like?

We know a lot about dinosaurs, but many things about them are still mysterious. These are some of the questions people often ask about dinosaurs:

Did dinosaurs have slit pupils?

Today's reptiles often have slit pupils, so in the past, drawings of dinosaurs showed them like that. But birds, which are related to dinosaurs, usually have round pupils.

The answer is that some dinosaurs probably did have slit pupils, which are often found among smaller predators that sometimes hunt at night. Others probably had round ones.

How do you tell the difference between male and female dinosaurs?

First, pick a small, peaceful dinosaur: trying to work out whether an *Albertosaurus* was male or female would be a terrible idea.

Second, don't bother. It is almost impossible to tell whether a dinosaur is female or male, at least based on their fossils. Experts have found a way to tell if a dinosaur was female, but only if she was pregnant when she died—and so far this has only been used for one *Tyrannosaurus* fossil.

What color was dinosaur blood?

Most of today's reptiles and all birds have red blood. Some creatures have different colored blood—for example, lobster blood is blue. However, dinosaurs almost certainly had red blood.

The idea of red dinosaur blood became more certain in 1991: long-dead red blood cells were actually found in the bones of *Tyrannosaurus*.

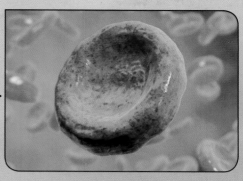

Did dinosaurs give birth to live babies or lay eggs?

Almost certainly, dinosaurs laid eggs, which then hatched just as birds' eggs do.

In 2008, though, experts discovered what they think is a baby, rather than an egg, inside a fossil *Dinocephalosaurus*. But this marine reptile was more closely related to marine crocodiles (rather than land dinosaurs) of 245 million years ago. These gave birth to live young, probably because they never left the water.

How far could a dinosaur travel?

Some dinosaurs probably never left their own area. Others seem to have moved to new locations as they followed migrating herds of prey, such as *Camarasaurus*, which was preyed on by *Ceratosaurus* and *Allosaurus*.

In fact, *Camarasaurus* probably traveled farthest and were the biggest dinosaurs to do so. During hot, dry summers, *Camarasaurus* moved from its usual floodplain territory to cooler uplands: a journey of around 180 miles (300 km) in each direction.

Index

The Author

Paul Mason is a prolific author of children's books, many award-nominated, on such subjects as 101 ways to save the planet, vile things that go wrong with the human body, and the world's looniest inventors. Many contain surprising, unbelievable, or just plain revolting facts. Today, he lives at a secret location on the coast of Europe, where his writing shack usually smells of drying wetsuit (he's a former international swimmer and a keen surfer).

The Illustrator

Andre Leonard trained at Camberwell art school in London and at Leicester University. He has illustrated prolifically for leading magazines and book publishers, and his paintings are in a number of private collections worldwide. Andre prefers to work digitally but sometimes combines this with traditional media. He lives in Stamford, UK, with his wife, children, and a cat called Kimi, and he loves flying and sailing.

Glossary

carnivorous: living on a diet mainly of meat. Carnivorous dinosaurs probably all hunted for food, though some may also have eaten already-dead animals.

delta: wide area of shallow water where a river flows into the sea or lake

Family: label given to groups of dinosaurs that had similar physical characteristics but were not exactly alike

fossil: remains of a living thing from long ago. Fossils can be the remains of bones, shells, pieces of wood, and plants—there are even fossilized footprints.

herbivorous: living on a diet of plants. Herbivorous dinosaurs would have been most plentiful wherever there was a good supply of plants and water.

herd: large group of animals, usually herbivorous, that band together for safety against predators

Order: one of two groups of dinosaurs, which were divided based on the way their hips worked

Ornithischia: one of the two orders of dinosaur. Ornithischian dinosaurs were "bird-hipped," with hips that looked similar to a bird's.

Saurischia: one of the two orders of dinosaur. Saurischian dinosaurs were "lizard-hipped," with hips that looked like a modern lizard's.

titanosaur: member of a group of lizard-hipped dinosaurs called sauropods. This group includes the biggest land animals that have ever existed.

Picture credits

t= top, b= bottom, l = left, m = middle, r = right.

Shutterstock: Aija Lehtonen 28mr; Catmando 28bl, 29tr; iurii 29br; Jaroslav Moravcik 31ml; Linda Bucklin 31br; nobeastsofierce 31tr; Pakhnyushchy 26t; plena 7tr; Pokpak Stock 30tr; Puwadol Jaturawutthichai 30m; Valentyna Chukhlyebova 28tl.